EMILY BRONTË

Selected Poems

BLOOMSBURY
★ POETRY ★
CLASSICS

St. Martin's Press
New York

Selection by Ian Hamilton
Jacket design by Jeff Fisher

ISBN 0-312-13438-X

First published in Great Britain by Bloomsbury Publishing Ltd.

10 9 8 7 6 5 4 3 2

CONTENTS

STARS

Ah! why, because the dazzling sun
    Restored our Earth to joy,
Have you departed, every one,
    And left a desert sky?

All through the night, your glorious eyes
    Were gazing down in mine,
And with a full heart's thankful sighs,
    I blessed that watch divine.

I was at peace, and drank your beams
    As they were life to me;
And revelled in my changeful dreams,
    Like petrel on the sea.

Thought followed thought, star followed star,
    Through boundless regions, on;
While one sweet influence, near and far,
    Thrilled through, and proved us one!

Why did the morning dawn to break
    So great, so pure, a spell;
And scorch with fire, the tranquil cheek,
    Where your cool radiance fell?

Blood-red, he rose, and, arrow-straight,
    His fierce beams struck my brow;
The soul of nature, sprang, elate,
    But *mine* sank sad and low!

My lids closed down, yet through their veil,
    I saw him, blazing, still,
And steep in gold the misty dale,
    And flash upon the hill.

I turned me to the pillow, then,
    To call back night, and see
Your worlds of solemn light, again,
    Throb with my heart, and me!

It would not do – the pillow glowed,
   And glowed both roof and floor;
And birds sang loudly in the wood,
   And fresh winds shook the door;

The curtains waved, the wakened flies
   Were murmuring round my room,
Imprisoned there, till I should rise,
   And give them leave to roam.

Oh, stars, and dreams, and gentle night;
   Oh, night and stars return!
And hide me from the hostile light,
   That does not warm, but burn;

That drains the blood of suffering men;
   Drinks tears, instead of dew;
Let me sleep through his blinding reign,
   And only wake with you!

REMEMBRANCE

Cold in the earth – and the deep snow piled above
   thee,
Far, far, removed, cold in the dreary grave!
Have I forgot, my only Love, to love thee,
Severed at last by Time's all-severing wave?

Now, when alone, do my thoughts no longer hover
Over the mountains, on that northern shore,
Resting their wings where heath and fern-leaves cover
Thy noble heart for ever, ever more?

Cold in the earth – and fifteen wild Decembers,
From those brown hills, have melted into spring:
Faithful, indeed, is the spirit that remembers
After such years of change and suffering!

Sweet Love of youth, forgive, if I forget thee,
While the world's tide is bearing me along;
Other desires and other hopes beset me,
Hopes which obscure, but cannot do thee wrong!

No later light has lightened up my heaven,
No second morn has ever shone for me;
All my life's bliss from thy dear life was given,
All my life's bliss is in the grave with thee.

But, when the days of golden dreams had perished,
And even Despair was powerless to destroy;
Then did I learn how existence could be cherished,
Strengthened, and fed without the aid of joy.

Then did I check the tears of useless passion –
Weaned my young soul from yearning after thine;
Sternly denied its burning wish to hasten
Down to that tomb already more than mine.

And, even yet, I dare not let it languish,
Dare not indulge in memory's rapturous pain;
Once drinking deep of that divinest anguish,
How could I seek the empty world again?

A DEATH-SCENE

'O Day! he cannot die
When thou so fair art shining!
O Sun, in such a glorious sky,
So tranquilly declining;

'He cannot leave thee now,
While fresh west winds are blowing,
And all around his youthful brow
Thy cheerful light is glowing!

'Edward, awake, awake –
The golden evening gleams
Warm and bright on Arden's lake –
Arouse thee from thy dreams!

'Beside thee, on my knee,
My dearest friend! I pray
That thou, to cross the eternal sea,
Wouldst yet one hour delay:

'I hear its billows roar –
I see them foaming high;
But no glimpse of a further shore
Has blest my straining eye.

'Believe not what they urge
Of Eden isles beyond;
Turn back, from that tempestuous surge,
To thy own native land.

'It is not death, but pain
That struggles in thy breast –
Nay, rally, Edward, rouse again;
I cannot let thee rest!'

One long look, that sore reproved me
For the woe I could not bear –
One mute look of suffering moved me
To repent my useless prayer:

And, with sudden check, the heaving
Of distraction passed away;
Not a sign of further grieving
Stirred my soul that awful day.

Paled, at length, the sweet sun setting;
Sunk to peace the twilight breeze:
Summer dews fell softly, wetting
Glen, and glade, and silent trees.

Then his eyes began to weary,
Weighed beneath a mortal sleep;
And their orbs grew strangely dreary,
Clouded, even as they would weep.

But they wept not, but they changed not,
Never moved, and never closed;
Troubled still, and still they ranged not –
Wandered not, nor yet reposed!

So I knew that he was dying –
Stooped, and raised his languid head;
Felt no breath, and heard no sighing,
So I knew that he was dead.

SONG

The linnet in the rocky dells,
  The moor-lark in the air,
The bee among the heather bells,
  That hide my lady fair:

The wild deer browse above her breast;
  The wild birds raise their brood;
And they, her smiles of love caressed,
  Have left her solitude!

I ween, that when the grave's dark wall
  Did first her form retain;
They thought their hearts could ne'er recall
  The light of joy again.

They thought the tide of grief would flow
  Unchecked through future years;
But where is all their anguish now,
  And where are all their tears?

Well, let them fight for honour's breath,
　　Or pleasure's shade pursue –
The dweller in the land of death
　　Is changed and careless too.

And, if their eyes should watch and weep
　　Till sorrow's source were dry,
　She would not, in her tranquil sleep,
　　Return a single sigh!

　Blow, west-wind, by the lonely mound,
　　And murmur, summer-streams –
There is no need of other sound
　　To soothe my lady's dreams.

ANTICIPATION

How beautiful the earth is still,
To thee – how full of happiness!
How little fraught with real ill,
Or unreal phantoms of distress!
How spring can bring thee glory, yet,
And summer win thee to forget
December's sullen time!
Why dost thou hold the treasure fast,
Of youth's delight, when youth is past,
    And thou art near thy prime?

When those who were thy own compeers,
Equals in fortune and in years,
Have seen their morning melt in tears,
    To clouded, smileless day;
Blest, had they died untried and young,
Before their hearts went wandering wrong,
Poor slaves, subdued by passions strong,
    A weak and helpless prey!

'Because, I hoped while they enjoyed,
And, by fulfilment, hope destroyed;
As children hope, with trustful breast,
I waited bliss – and cherished rest.
A thoughtful spirit taught me, soon,
That we must long till life be done;
That every phase of earthly joy
Must always fade, and always cloy:

'This I foresaw – and would not chase
   The fleeting treacheries;
But, with firm foot and tranquil face,
Held backward from that tempting race,
Gazed o'er the sands the waves efface,
   To the enduring seas –
There cast my anchor of desire
Deep in unknown eternity;
Nor ever let my spirit tire,
With looking for *what is to be!*

'It is hope's spell that glorifies,
Like youth, to my maturer eyes,
All Nature's million mysteries,
    The fearful and the fair –
Hope soothes me in the griefs I know;
She lulls my pain for others' woe,
And makes me strong to undergo
    What I am born to bear.

'Glad comforter! will I not brave,
Unawed, the darkness of the grave?
Nay, smile to hear Death's billows rave –
    Sustained, my guide, by thee?
The more unjust seems present fate,
The more my spirit swells elate,
Strong, in thy strength, to anticipate
    Rewarding destiny!'

THE PRISONER (A FRAGMENT)

In the dungeon-crypts, idly did I stray,
Reckless of the lives wasting there away;
'Draw the ponderous bars! open, Warder stern!'
He dared not say me nay – the hinges harshly turn.

'Our guests are darkly lodged,' I whisper'd, gazing
  through
The vault, whose grated eye showed heaven more grey
  than blue;
(This was when glad spring laughed in awaking pride;)
'Aye, darkly lodged enough!' returned my sullen guide.

Then, God forgive my youth; forgive my careless
  tongue;
I scoffed, as chill chains on the damp flag-stones rung:
'Confined in triple walls, art thou so much to fear,
That we must bind thee down and clench thy fetters
  here?'

The captive raised her face, it was as soft and mild
As sculptured marble saint, or slumbering unwean'd
  child;
It was so soft and mild, it was so sweet and fair,
Pain could not trace a line, nor grief a shadow there!

The captive raised her hand and pressed it to her
    brow;
'I have been struck,' she said, 'and I am suffering now;
Yet these are little worth, your bolts and irons strong,
And, were they forged in steel, they could not hold
    me long.'

Hoarse laughed the jailer grim: 'Shall I be won to
    hear;
Dost think, fond, dreaming wretch, that *I* shall grant
    thy prayer?
Or, better still, wilt melt my master's heart with
    groans?
Ah! sooner might the sun thaw down these granite
    stones.

'My master's voice is low, his aspect bland and kind,
But hard as hardest flint, the soul that lurks behind;
And I am rough and rude, yet not more rough to see
Than is the hidden ghost that has its home in me.'

About her lips there played a smile of almost scorn,
'My friend,' she gently said, 'you have not heard me
    mourn;
When you my kindred's lives, *my* lost life, can restore,
Then may I weep and sue, – but never, friend, before!

'Still, let my tyrants know, I am not doomed to wear
Year after year in gloom, and desolate despair;
A messenger of Hope, comes every night to me,
And offers for short life, eternal liberty.

'He comes with western winds, with evening's
    wandering airs,
With that clear dusk of heaven that brings the thickest
    stars.
Winds take a pensive tone, and stars a tender fire,
And visions rise, and change, that kill me with desire.

'Desire for nothing known in my maturer years,
When Joy grew mad with awe, at counting future
    tears.
When, if my spirit's sky was full of flashes warm,
I knew not whence they came, from sun, or thunder
    storm.

'But, first, a hush of peace – a soundless calm
    descends;
The struggle of distress, and fierce impatience ends.
Mute music soothes my breast, unuttered harmony,
That I could never dream, till Earth was lost to me.

'Then dawns the Invisible; the Unseen its truth
  reveals;
My outward sense is gone, my inward essence feels:
Its wings are almost free – its home, its harbour found,
Measuring the gulf, it stoops, and dares the final
  bound.

'Oh, dreadful is the check – intense the agony –
When the ear begins to hear, and the eye begins to
  see;
When the pulse begins to throb, the brain to think
  again,
The soul to feel the flesh, and the flesh to feel the
  chain.

'Yet I would lose no sting, would wish no torture less,
The more that anguish racks, the earlier it will bless;
And robed in fires of hell, or bright with heavenly
  shine,
If it but herald death, the vision is divine!'

She ceased to speak, and we, unanswering, turned to
  go –
We had no further power to work the captive woe:
Her cheek, her gleaming eye, declared that man had
  given
A sentence, unapproved, and overruled by Heaven.

HOPE

Hope was but a timid friend;
　　She sat without the grated den,
Watching how my fate would tend,
　　Even as selfish-hearted men.

She was cruel in her fear;
　　Through the bars, one dreary day,
I looked out to see her there,
　　And she turned her face away!

Like a false guard, false watch keeping,
　　Still in strife, she whispered peace;
She would sing while I was weeping;
　　If I listened, she would cease.

False she was, and unrelenting;
　　When my last joys strewed the ground,
Even Sorrow saw, repenting,
　　Those sad relics scattered round;

Hope, whose whisper would have given
　　Balm to all my frenzied pain,
Stretched her wings, and soared to heaven,
　　Went, and ne'er returned again!

A DAY DREAM

On a sunny brae, alone I lay
   One summer afternoon;
It was the marriage-time of May
   With her young lover, June.

From her mother's heart, seemed loath to part
   That queen of bridal charms,
But her father smiled on the fairest child
   He ever held in his arms.

The trees did wave their plumy crests,
   The glad birds carolled clear;
And I, of all the wedding guests,
   Was only sullen there!

There was not one, but wished to shun
   My aspect void of cheer;
The very grey rocks, looking on,
   Asked, 'What do you here?'

And I could utter no reply;
   In sooth, I did not know
Why I had brought a clouded eye
   To greet the general glow.

So, resting on a heathy bank,
    I took my heart to me;
And we together sadly sank
    Into a reverie.

We thought, 'When winter comes again,
    Where will these bright things be?
All vanished, like a vision vain,
    An unreal mockery!

'The birds that now so blithely sing,
    Through deserts, frozen dry,
Poor spectres of the perished spring,
    In famished troops, will fly.

TO IMAGINATION

When weary with the long day's care,
  And earthly change from pain to pain,
And lost and ready to despair,
  Thy kind voice calls me back again:
Oh, my true friend! I am not lone,
While thou canst speak with such a tone!

So hopeless is the world without;
  The world within I doubly prize;
Thy world, where guile, and hate, and doubt,
  And cold suspicion never rise;
Where thou, and I, and Liberty,
Have undisputed sovereignty.

What matters it, that, all around,
  Danger, and guilt, and darkness lie,
If but within our bosom's bound
  We hold a bright, untroubled sky,
Warm with ten thousand mingled rays
Of suns that know no winter days?

Reason, indeed, may oft complain
    For Nature's sad reality,
And tell the suffering heart how vain
    Its cherished dreams must always be;
And Truth may rudely trample down
The flowers of Fancy, newly-blown:

But, thou art ever there, to bring
    The hovering vision back, and breathe
New glories o'er the blighted spring,
    And call a lovelier Life from Death,
And whisper, with a voice divine,
Of real worlds, as bright as thine.

I trust not to thy phantom bliss,
    Yet, still, in evening's quiet hour,
With never-failing thankfulness,
    I welcome thee, Benignant Power;
Sure solacer of human cares,
And sweeter hope, when hope despairs!

HOW CLEAR SHE SHINES

How clear she shines! How quietly
   I lie beneath her guardian light;
While heaven and earth are whispering me,
   'Tomorrow, wake, but, dream tonight.'
Yes, Fancy, come, my Fairy love!
   These throbbing temples softly kiss;
And bend my lonely couch above
   And bring me rest, and bring me bliss.

The world is going; dark world, adieu!
   Grim world, conceal thee till the day;
The heart, thou canst not all subdue,
   Must still resist, if thou delay!

Thy love I will not, will not share;
   Thy hatred only wakes a smile;
Thy griefs may wound – thy wrongs may tear,
   But, oh, thy lies shall ne'er beguile!
While gazing on the stars that glow
   Above me, in that stormless sea,
I long to hope that all the woe
   Creation knows, is held in thee!

And this shall be my dream tonight;
  I'll think the heaven of glorious spheres
Is rolling on its course of light
  In endless bliss, through endless years;
I'll think, there's not one world above,
  Far as these straining eyes can see,
Where wisdom ever laughed at Love,
  Or Virtue crouched to Infamy;

Where, writhing 'neath the strokes of Fate,
  The mangled wretch was forced to smile;
To match his patience 'gainst her hate,
  His heart rebellious all the while.
Where Pleasure still will lead to wrong,
  And helpless Reason warn in vain;
And Truth is weak, and Treachery strong;
  And Joy the surest path to Pain;
And Peace, the lethargy of Grief;
  And Hope, a phantom of the soul;
And Life, a labour, void and brief;
  And Death, the despot of the whole!

SYMPATHY

There should be no despair for you
  While nightly stars are burning;
While evening pours its silent dew
  And sunshine gilds the morning.
There should be no despair – though tears
  May flow down like a river:
Are not the best beloved of years
  Around your heart for ever?

They weep, you weep, it must be so;
  Winds sigh as you are sighing,
And Winter sheds his grief in snow
  Where Autumn's leaves are lying:
Yet, these revive, and from their fate
  Your fate cannot be parted:
Then, journey on, if not elate,
  Still, *never* broken-hearted!

PLEAD FOR ME

Oh, thy bright eyes must answer now,
When Reason, with a scornful brow,
Is mocking at my overthrow!
Oh, thy sweet tongue must plead for me
And tell, why I have chosen thee!

Stern Reason is to judgment come,
Arrayed in all her forms of gloom:
Wilt thou, my advocate, be dumb?
No, radiant angel, speak and say,
Why I did cast the world away.

Why I have persevered to shun
The common paths that others run,
And on a strange road journeyed on,
Heedless, alike, of wealth and power –
Of glory's wreath and pleasure's flower.

These, once, indeed, seemed Beings Divine;
And they, perchance, heard vows of mine,
And saw my offerings on their shrine;
But, careless gifts are seldom prized,
And *mine* were worthily despised.

So, with a ready heart I swore
To seek their altar-stone no more;
And gave my spirit to adore
Thee, ever-present, phantom thing;
My slave, my comrade, and my king,

A slave, because I rule thee still;
Incline thee to my changeful will,
And make thy influence good or ill:
A comrade, for by day and night
Thou art my intimate delight, –

My darling pain that wounds and sears
And wrings a blessing out from tears
By deadening me to earthly cares;
And yet, a king, though Prudence well
Have taught thy subject to rebel.

And am I wrong to worship, where
Faith cannot doubt, nor hope despair,
Since my own soul can grant my prayer?
Speak, God of visions, plead for me,
And tell why I have chosen thee!

SELF-INTERROGATION

'The evening passes fast away,
    'Tis almost time to rest;
What thoughts has left the vanished day,
    What feelings, in thy breast?'

'The vanished day? It leaves a sense
    Of labour hardly done;
Of little, gained with vast expense, –
    A sense of grief alone!

'Time stands before the door of Death,
    Upbraiding bitterly;
And Conscience, with exhaustless breath,
    Pours black reproach on me:

'And though I've said that Conscience lies,
    And Time should Fate condemn;
Still, sad Repentance clouds my eyes,
    And makes me yield to them!'

DEATH

Death! that struck when I was most confiding
In my certain faith of joy to be –
Strike again, Time's withered branch dividing
From the fresh root of Eternity!

Leaves, upon Time's branch, were growing brightly,
Full of sap, and full of silver dew;
Birds beneath its shelter gathered nightly;
Daily round its flowers the wild bees flew.

Sorrow passed, and plucked the golden blossom;
Guilt stripped off the foliage in its pride;
But, within its parent's kindly bosom,
Flowed for ever Life's restoring tide.

Little mourned I for the parted gladness,
For the vacant nest and silent song –
Hope was there, and laughed me out of sadness;
Whispering, 'Winter will not linger long!'

And, behold! with tenfold increase blessing,
Spring adorned the beauty-burdened spray;
Wind and rain and fervent heat, caressing,
Lavished glory on that second May!

High it rose – no winged grief could sweep it;
Sin was scared to distance with its shine;
Love, and its own life, had power to keep it
From all wrong – from every blight but thine!

Cruel Death! The young leaves droop and languish;
Evening's gentle air may still restore –
No! the morning sunshine mocks my anguish –
Time, for me, must never blossom more!

Strike it down, that other boughs may flourish
Where that perished sapling used to be;
Thus, at least, its mouldering corpse will nourish
That from which it sprung – Eternity.

STANZAS TO –

Well, some may hate, and some may scorn,
And some may quite forget thy name;
But my sad heart must ever mourn
Thy ruined hopes, thy blighted fame!
'Twas thus I thought, an hour ago,
Even weeping o'er that wretch's woe;
One word turned back my gushing tears,
And lit my altered eye with sneers.
Then 'Bless the friendly dust,' I said,
'That hides thy unlamented head!
Vain as thou wert, and weak as vain,
The slave of Falsehood, Pride, and Pain, –
My heart has nought akin to thine;
Thy soul is powerless over mine.'

But these were thoughts that vanished too;
Unwise, unholy, and untrue:
Do I despise the timid deer,
Because his limbs are fleet with fear?
Or, would I mock the wolf's death-howl,
Because his form is gaunt and foul?
Or, hear with joy the leveret's cry,
Because it cannot bravely die?
No! Then above his memory
Let Pity's heart as tender be;
Say, 'Earth, lie lightly on that breast
And, kind Heaven, grant that spirit rest!'

HONOUR'S MARTYR

The moon is full this winter night;
   The stars are clear, though few;
And every window glistens bright,
   With leaves of frozen dew.

The sweet moon through your lattice gleams
   And lights your room like day;
And there you pass, in happy dreams,
   The peaceful hours away!

While I, with effort hardly quelling
   The anguish in my breast,
Wander about the silent dwelling,
   And cannot think of rest.

The old clock in the gloomy hall
   Ticks on, from hour to hour;
And every time its measured call
   Seems lingering slow and slower:

And oh, how slow that keen-eyed star
   Has tracked the chilly grey!
What, watching yet! how very far
   The morning lies away!

Without your chamber door I stand;
   Love, are you slumbering still?
My cold heart, underneath my hand,
   Has almost ceased to thrill.

Bleak, bleak the east wind sobs and sighs,
   And drowns the turret bell,
Whose sad note, undistinguished, dies
   Unheard, like my farewell!

Tomorrow, Scorn will blight my name,
   And Hate will trample me,
Will load me with a coward's shame –
   A traitor's perjury.

False friends will launch their covert sneers;
  True friends will wish me dead;
And I shall cause the bitterest tears
  That you have ever shed.

The dark deeds of my outlawed race
  Will then like virtues shine;
And men will pardon their disgrace,
  Beside the guilt of mine.

For, who forgives the accursed crime
  Of dastard treachery?
Rebellion, in its chosen time,
  May Freedom's champion be;

Revenge may stain a righteous sword,
  It may be just to slay;
But, traitor, traitor, – from *that* word
  All true breasts shrink away!

Oh, I would give my heart to death,
    To keep my honour fair;
Yet, I'll not give my inward faith
    My honour's *name* to spare!

Not even to keep your priceless love,
    Dare I, Beloved, deceive;
This treason should the future prove,
    Then, only then, believe!

I know the path I ought to go;
    I follow fearlessly,
Inquiring not what deeper woe
    Stern duty stores for me.

So foes pursue, and cold allies
    Mistrust me, every one:
Let me be false in others' eyes,
    If faithful in my own.

STANZAS

I'll not weep that thou art going to leave me,
  There's nothing lovely here;
And doubly will the dark world grieve me,
  While thy heart suffers there.

I'll not weep, because the summer's glory
  Must always end in gloom;
And, follow out the happiest story –
  It closes with a tomb!

And I am weary of the anguish
  Increasing winters bear;
Weary to watch the spirit languish
  Through years of dead despair.

So, if a tear, when thou art dying,
  Should haply fall from me,
It is but that my soul is sighing,
  To go and rest with thee.

MY COMFORTER

Well hast thou spoken, and yet, not taught
   A feeling strange or new;
Thou hast but roused a latent thought,
A cloud-closed beam of sunshine, brought
   To gleam in open view.

Deep down, concealed within my soul,
   That light lies hid from men;
Yet, glows unquenched – though shadows roll,
Its gentle ray cannot control,
   About the sullen den.

Was I not vexed, in these gloomy ways
   To walk alone so long?
Around me, wretches uttering praise,
Or howling o'er their hopeless days,
   And each with Frenzy's tongue; –

A brotherhood of misery,
   Their smiles as sad as sighs;
Whose madness daily maddened me,
Distorting into agony
   The bliss before my eyes!

So stood I, in Heaven's glorious sun,
    And in the glare of Hell;
My spirit drank a mingled tone,
Of seraph's song, and demon's moan;
What my soul bore, my soul alone
    Within itself may tell!

Like a soft air, above a sea,
    Tossed by the tempest's stir;
A thaw-wind, melting quietly
The snow-drift, on some wintry lea;
No: what sweet thing resembles thee,
    My thoughtful Comforter?

And yet a little longer speak,
    Calm this resentful mood;
And while the savage heart grows meek,
For other token do not seek,
But let the tear upon my cheek
    Evince my gratitude!

THE OLD STOIC

Riches I hold in light esteem;
   And Love I laugh to scorn;
And lust of fame was but a dream
   That vanished with the morn:

And if I pray, the only prayer
   That moves my lips for me
Is, 'Leave the heart that now I bear,
   And give me liberty!'

Yes, as my swift days near their goal,
   'Tis all that I implore;
In life and death, a chainless soul,
   With courage to endure.

TELL ME TELL ME

Tell me tell me smiling child
What the past is like to thee?
An Autumn evening soft and mild
With a wind that sighs mournfully

Tell me what is the present hour?
A green and flowery spray
Where a young bird sits gathering its power
To mount and fly away

And what is the future happy one?
A sea beneath a cloudless sun
A mighty glorious dazzling sea
Stretching into infinity

START NOT UPON THE MINSTER WALL

Start not upon the minster wall
Sunshine is shed in holy calm
And lonely though my footsteps fall
The saints shall shelter thee from harm

Shrink not if it be summer noon
This shadow should right welcome be
These stairs are steep but landed soon
We'll rest us long and quietly

What though our path be o'er the dead
They slumber soundly in the tomb
And why should mortals fear to tread
The pathway to their future home?

REDBREAST EARLY

Redbreast early in the morning
Dark and cold and cloudy grey
Wildly tender is thy music
Chasing the angry thoughts away

* * *

My heart is not enraptured now
My eyes are full of tears
And constant sorrow on my brow
Has done the work of years

It was not hope that wrecked at once
The spirit's early storm
But a long life of solitude
Hopes quenched and rising thoughts subdued
A bleak November's calm

* * *

What woke it then? A little child
Strayed from its father's cottage door
And in the hour of moonlight mild
Laid lonely on the desert moor

* * *

I heard it then you heard it too
And seraph sweet it sang to you
But like the shriek of misery
That wild wild music wailed to me

THERE SHINES THE MOON

There shines the moon, at noon of night –
Vision of glory – Dream of light!
Holy as heaven – undimmed and pure,
Looking down on the lonely moor –
And lonelier still beneath her ray
That drear moor stretches far away
Till it seems strange that aught can lie
Beyond its zone of silver sky –

Bright moon – dear moon! when years have past
My weary feet return at last –
And still upon Lake Elnor's breast
Thy solemn rays serenely rest
And still the Fern-leaves sighing wave
Like mourners over Elbë's grave
And Earth's the same but Oh to see
How wildly Time has altered me!
Am I the being who long ago
Sat watching by that water side
The light of life expiring slow
From his fair cheek and brow of pride?
Not oft these mountains feel the shine
Of such a day – as fading then,
Cast from its fount of gold divine
A last smile on the heathery plain
And kissed the far-off peaks of snow
That gleaming on the horizon shone

As if in summer's warmest glow
Stern winter claimed a loftier throne –
And there he lay among the bloom
His red blood dyed a deeper hue
Shuddering to feel the ghostly gloom
That coming Death around him threw –
Sickening to think one hour would sever
The sweet, sweet world and him forever
To think that twilight gathering dim
Would never pass away to him –
No – never more! That awful thought
A thousand dreary feelings brought,
And memory all her powers combined
And rushed upon his fainting mind.
Wide, swelling woodlands seemed to rise
Beneath soft, sunny, southern skies –
Old Elbë Hall his noble home
Towered 'mid its trees, whose foliage green
Rustled with the kind airs that come
From summer Heavens when most serene
And bursting through the leafy shade
A gush of golden sunshine played;
Bathing the walls in amber light
And sparkling in the water clear
That stretched below – reflected bright
The whole wide world of cloudless air –
And still before his spirit's eye
Such well known scenes would rise and fly
Till, maddening with despair and pain

He turned his dying face to me
And wildly cried, 'Oh once again
Might I my native country see!
But once again – one single day!
And must it – can it *never* be?
To die – and die so far away
When life has hardly smiled for me –
Augusta – you will soon return
Back to that land in health and bloom
And then the heath alone will mourn
Above my unremembered tomb
For you'll forget the lonely grave
And mouldering corpse by Elnor's wave' –

THE NIGHT OF STORMS

The night of storms has passed
The sunshine bright and clear
Gives glory to the verdant waste
And warms the breezy air

And I would leave my bed
Its cheering smile to see
To chase the visions from my head
Whose forms have troubled me

In all the hours of gloom
My soul was rapt away
I dreamt I stood by a marble tomb
Where royal corpses lay

It was just the time of eve
When parted ghosts might come
Above their prisoned dust to grieve
And wail their woeful doom

And truly at my side
I saw a shadowy thing
Most dim and yet its presence there
Curdled my blood with ghastly fear
And ghastlier wondering

My breath I could not draw
The air seemed ranny
But still my eyes with maddening gaze
Were fixed upon its fearful face
And its were fixed on me

I fell down on the stone
But could not turn away
My words died in a voiceless moan
When I began to pray

And still it bent above
Its features full in view
It seemed close by and yet more far
Than this world from the farthest star
That tracks the boundless blue

Indeed 'twas not the space
Of earth or time between
But the sea of death's eternity
The gulf o'er which mortality
Has never never been

O bring not back again
The horror of that hour
When its lips opened and a sound
Awoke the stillness reigning round
Faint as a dream but the earth shrank
And heaven's lights shivered 'neath its power

'Woe for the day Regina's pride
Regina's hope is in the grave
And who shall rule my land beside
And who shall save

'Woe for the day with gory tears
My country's sons this day shall rue
Woe for the day a thousand years
Can not repair what one shall do

'Woe for the day' mixed with the wind
That sad lament was ringing
It almost broke my heart to hear
Such dreary dreary singing

I SAW THEE CHILD

I saw thee child one summer's day
Suddenly leave thy cheerful play
And in the green grass lowly lying
I listened to thy mournful sighing

I knew the wish that waked that wail
I knew the source whence sprung those tears
You longed for fate to raise the veil
That darkened over coming years

The anxious prayer was heard and power
Was given me in that silent hour
To open to an infant's eye
The portals of futurity

But child of dust the fragrant flowers
The bright blue sky and velvet sod
Were strange conductors to the bowers
Thy daring footsteps must have trod

I watched my time and summer passed
And Autumn waning fleeted by
And doleful winter nights at last
In cloudy mourning clothed the sky

And now I'm come this evening fell
Not stormily but stilly drear
A sound sweeps o'er thee like a knell
To banish joy and welcome care

A fluttering blast that shakes the leaves
And whistles round the gloomy wall
And lingering long lamenting grieves
For 'tis the spectre's call

He hears me what a sudden start
Sent the blood icy to that heart
He wakens and how ghastly white
That face looks in the dim lamplight

Those tiny hands in vain essay
To thrust the shadowy fiend away
There is a horror on his brow
An anguish in his bosom now

A fearful anguish in his eyes
Fixed strainedly on the vacant air
Heavily bursts in long drawn sighs
His panting breath enchained by fear

Poor child if spirits such as I
Could weep o'er human misery
A tear might flow aye many a tear
To see the road that lies before
To see the sunshine disappear
And hear the stormy waters roar
Breaking upon a desolate shore
Cut off from hope in early day
From power and glory cut away
But it is doomed and morning's light
Must image forth the scowl of night
And childhood's flower must waste its bloom
Beneath the shadow of the tomb

O GOD OF HEAVEN

O God of heaven! the dream of horror
The frightful dream is over now
The sickened heart the blasting sorrow
The ghastly night the ghastlier morrow
The aching sense of utter woe.

The burning tears that would keep welling
The groans that mocked at every tear
That burst from out their dreary dwelling
As if each gasp were life expelling
But life was nourished by despair

The tossing and the anguished pining
The grinding teeth and staring eye
The agony of still repining
When not a spark of hope was shining
From gloomy fate's relentless sky

The impatient rage the useless shrinking
From thoughts that yet could not be borne
The soul that was for ever thinking
Till nature maddened tortured sinking
At last refused to mourn –

It's over now – and I am free
And the ocean wind is caressing me
The wild wind from that wavy main
I never thought to see again

Bless thee Bright Sea – and glorious dome
And my own world my spirit's home
Bless thee – Bless all – I can not speak
My voice is choked, but not with grief
And salt drops from my haggard cheek
Descend like rain upon the heath

How long they've wet a dungeon floor –
Falling on flag-stones damp and grey
I used to weep even in my sleep
The night was dreadful like the day

I used to weep when winter's snow
Whirled through the grating stormily
But then it was a calmer woe
For every thing was drear as me

The bitterest time the worst of all
Was that in which the summer sheen
Cast a green lustre on the wall
That told of Fields of lovelier green

Often I've sat down on the ground
Gazing up to that flush scarce seen
Till heedless of the darkness round
My soul has sought a land serene

It sought the arch of heaven divine
The pure blue heaven with clouds of gold
It sought thy Father's home and mine
As I remembered it of old

O even now too horribly
Come back the feelings that would swell
When with my face hid on my knee
I strove the bursting groans to quell

I flung myself upon the stone
I howled and tore my tangled hair
And then when the first gush had flown
Lay in unspeakable despair

Sometimes a curse sometimes a prayer
Would quiver on my parched tongue
But both without a murmur there
Died in the breast from whence they sprung

And so the day would fade on high
And darkness quench that lonely beam
And slumber mould my misery
Into some strange and spectral dream
Whose phantom horrors made me know
The worst extent of human woe –

But this is past and why return
O'er such a past to brood and mourn?
Shake off the fetters break the chain
And live and love and smile again

The waste of youth the waste of years
Departed in that dungeon's thrall
The gnawing grief the hopeless tears
Forget them – O forget them all –

THE BATTLE HAD PASSED

The battle had passed from the height
And still did evening fall
While heaven with its hosts of night
Gloriously canopied all

The dead around were sleeping
On heath and granite grey
And the dying their last watch were keeping
In the closing of the day

* * *

How golden bright from earth and heaven
The summer day declines
How gloriously o'er land and sea
The parting sunbeam shines

There is a voice in the wind that waves
Those bright rejoicing trees

* * *

Not a vapour had stained the breezeless blue
Not a cloud had dimmed the sun
From the time of morning's earliest dew
Till the summer day was done

And all as pure and all as bright
The beam of evening died
And purer still its parting light
Shone in Lake Elnor's tide

Waveless and calm lies that silent deep
In its wilderness of moors
Solemn and soft the moonbeams sleep
Upon its heathy shores

The deer are gathered to their rest
The wild sheep seek the fold

*　*　*

Only some spires of bright green grass
Transparently in sunshine quivering

THE SUN HAS SET

The sun has set and the long grass now
Waves drearily in the evening wind
And the wild bird has flown from that old grey stone
In some warm nook a couch to find

In all the lonely landscape round
I see no sight and hear no sound
Except the wind that far away
Comes sighing o'er the heathy sea

AND FIRST AN HOUR

And first an hour of mournful musing
And then a gush of bitter tears
And then a dreary calm diffusing
Its deadly mist o'er joys and cares

And then a throb and then a lightening
And then a breathing from above
And then a star in heaven brightening
The star the glorious star of love

LONG NEGLECT

Long neglect has worn away
Half the sweet enchanting smile
Time has turned the bloom to grey
Mould and damp the face defile

But that lock of silky hair
Still beneath the picture twined
Tells what once those features were
Paints their image on the mind

Fair the hand that traced that line
'Dearest ever deem me true'
Swiftly flew the fingers fine
When the pen that motto drew

ALONE I SAT

Alone I sat the summer day
Had died in smiling light away
I saw it die I watched it fade
From misty hill and breezeless glade

And thoughts in my soul were rushing
And my heart bowed beneath their power
And tears within my eyes were gushing
Because I could not speak the feeling
The solemn joy around me stealing
In that divine untroubled hour

I asked my self O why has heaven
Denied the precious gift to me
The glorious gift to many given
To speak their thoughts in poetry

Dreams have encircled me I said
From careless childhood's sunny time
Visions by ardent fancy fed
Since life was in its morning prime

But now when I had hoped to sing
My fingers strike a tuneless string
And still the burden of the strain
Is strive no more 'tis all in vain

A.G.A. TO A.E.

Lord of Elbë, on Elbë hill
The mist is thick and the wind is chill
And the heart of thy Friend from the dawn of day
Has sighed for sorrow that thou went away –

Lord of Elbë, how pleasant to me
The sound of thy blithesome step would be
Rustling the heath that, only now
Waves as the night-gusts over it blow

Bright are the fires in thy lonely home
I see them far off, and as deepens the gloom
Gleaming like stars through the high forest-boughs
Gladder they glow in the park's repose –

O Alexander! when I return,
Warm as those hearths my heart would burn,
Light as thine own, my foot would fall
If I might hear thy voice in the hall –

But thou art now on a desolate sea –
Parted from Gondal and parted from me –
All my repining is hopeless and vain,
Death never yields back his victims again –

SLEEP BRINGS NO JOY

Sleep brings no joy to me
Remembrance never dies
My soul is given to misery
And lives in sighs

Sleep brings no rest to me
The shadows of the dead
My waking eyes may never see
Surround my bed

Sleep brings no hope to me
In soundest sleep they come
And with their doleful imagery
Deepen the gloom

Sleep brings no strength to me
No power renewed to brave
I only sail a wilder sea
A darker wave

Sleep brings no friend to me
To soothe and aid to bear
They all gaze on how scornfully
And I despair

Sleep brings no wish to knit
My harassed heart beneath
My only wish is to forget
In the sleep of death

THE NIGHT IS DARKENING

The night is darkening round me
The wild winds coldly blow
But a tyrant spell has bound me
And I cannot cannot go

The giant trees are bending
Their bare boughs weighed with snow
And the storm is fast descending
And yet I cannot go

Clouds beyond clouds above me
Wastes beyond wastes below
But nothing drear can move me
I will not cannot go

I'll come when thou art saddest
Laid alone in the darkened room
When the mad day's mirth has vanished
And the smile of joy is banished
From evening's chilly gloom

I'll come when the heart's real feeling
Has entire unbiased sway
And my influence o'er thee stealing
Grief deepening joy congealing
Shall bear thy soul away

Listen 'tis just the hour
The awful time for thee
Dost thou not feel upon thy soul
A flood of strange sensations roll
Forerunners of a sterner power
Heralds of me

I would have touched the heavenly key
That spoke alike of bliss and thee
I would have woke the entrancing song
But its words died upon my tongue
And then I knew that hallowed strain
Could never speak of joy again
And then I felt

LINES

I die but when the grave shall press
The heart so long endeared to thee
When earthly cares no more distress
And earthly joys are nought to me

Weep not, but think that I have past
Before thee o'er a sea of gloom
Have anchored safe and rest at last
Where tears and mourning cannot come

'Tis I should weep to leave thee here
On that dark Ocean sailing drear
With storms around and fears before
And no kind light to point the shore

But long or short though life may be
'Tis nothing to eternity
We part below to meet on high
Where blissful ages never die

O MOTHER

O mother I am not regretting
To leave this wretched world below
If there be nothing but forgetting
In that dark land to which I go

Yet though 'tis wretched now to languish
Deceived and tired and hopeless here
No heart can quite repress the anguish
Of leaving things that once were dear

Twice twelve short years and all is over
And day and night to rise no more
And never more to be a rover
Along the fields the woods the shore

And never more at early dawning
To watch the stars of midnight wane
To breathe the breath of summer morning
And see its sunshine ne'er again

I hear the Abbey bells are ringing
Methinks their chime sound faint and drear
Or else the wind is adverse winging
And wafts its music from my ear

The wind the winter night is speaking
Of thoughts and things that should not stay
Mother come near my heart is breaking
I cannot bear to go away

And I *must* go whence no returning
To soothe your grief or calm your care
Nay do not weep that bitter mourning
Tortures my soul with wild despair

No tell me that when I am lying
In the old church beneath the stone
You'll dry your tears and check your sighing
And soon forget the spirit gone

You've asked me long to tell what sorrow
Has blanched my cheek and quenched my eye
And we shall sever ere tomorrow
So I'll confess before I die

Ten years ago in last September
Fernando left his home and you
And still I think you must remember
The anguish of that last adieu

And well you know how wildly pining
I longed to see his face again
Through all the Autumn's drear declining
Its stormy nights and days of rain

Down on the skirts of Areon's forest
There lies a lone and lovely glade
And there the hearts together nourished
Their first their fatal parting made

The afternoon in softened glory
So Bathed each green swell and waving tree
Beyond the broad park spread before me
Stretched far away the boundless sea

And there I stood when he had left me
With ashy cheek but tearless eye
Watching the ship whose sail bereft me
Of life and hope and peace and joy

It past that night I sought a pillow
Of sleepless woe and grieving lone
My soul still hovered o'er the billow
And mourned a love for ever flown

Yet smiling bright in recollection
One blissful hour returns to me
One letter told of firm affection
Of safe deliverance from the sea

But not another fearing hoping
Spring winter harvest glided o'er
And time at length brought power for coping
With thoughts I could not once endure

And I would seek in summer's evening
The place that saw our last farewell
And there a chain of visions weaving
I'd linger till the curfew bell

O EVENING WHY

O evening why is thy light so sad?
Why is the sun's last ray so cold
Hush our smile is as ever glad
But thy heart is growing old

It's over now I've known it all
I'll hide it in my heart no more
But back again that night recall
And think the fearful vision o'er

The evening sun in cloudless shine
Had passed from summer's heaven divine
And dark the shades of twilight grew
And stars were in the depth of blue

And in the heath on mountains far
From human eye and human care
With thoughtful heart and tearful eye
I sadly watched that solemn sky

HARP

Harp of wild and dream like strain
When I touch thy strings
Why dost thou repeat again
Long forgotten things?

Harp in other earlier days
I could sing to thee
And not one of all my lays
Vexed my memory

But now if I awake a note
That gave me joy before
Sounds of sorrow from thee float
Changing evermore

Yet still steeped in memory's dyes
They come sailing on
Darkening all my summer skies
Shutting out my sun

WHY DO I HATE

Why do I hate that lone green dell?
Buried in moors and mountains wild
That is a spot I had loved too well
Had I but seen it when a child

There are bones whitening there in the summer's heat
But it is not for that and none can tell
None but one can the secret repeat
Why I hate that lone green dell

Noble foe I pardon thee
All thy cold and scornful pride
For thou wast a priceless friend to me
When my sad heart had none beside

And leaning on thy generous arm
A breath of old times over me came
The earth shone round with a long lost charm
Alas I forgot I was not the same

Before a day – an hour passed by
My spirit knew itself once more
I saw the gilded vapours fly
And leave me as I was before

A.G.A. TO A.S.

O wander not so far away!
O love, forgive this selfish tear.
It may be sad for thee to stay
But how can I live lonely here?

The still May morn is warm and bright
Young flowers look fresh and grass is green
And in the haze of glorious light
Our long low hills are scarcely seen –

The woods – even now their small leaves hide
The blackbird and the stockdove well
And high in heaven so blue and wide
A thousand strains of music swell –

He looks on all with eyes that speak
So deep, so drear a woe to me!
There is a faint red on his cheek
Not like the bloom I used to see.

Can Death – yes, Death, he is thine own!
The grave must close those limbs around
And hush, for ever hush the tone
I loved above all earthly sound.

Well, pass away with the other flowers
Too dark for them, too dark for thee
Are the hours to come, the joyless hours
That Time is treasuring up for me.

If thou hast sinned in this world of care
'Twas but the dust of thy drear abode –
Thy soul was pure when it entered here
And pure it will go again to God –

GLENEDEN'S DREAM

Tell me, watcher, is it winter?
Say how long my sleep has been?
Have the woods I left so lovely,
Lost their robes of tender green?

Is the morning slow in coming?
Is the nighttime loath to go?
Tell me, are the dreary mountains
Drearier still with drifted snow?

'Captive, since thou sawest the forest
All its leaves have died away
And another March has woven
Garlands for another May –

'Ice has barred the Arctic water,
Soft south winds have set it free
And once more to deep green valley
Golden flowers might welcome thee' –

Watcher, in this lonely prison,
Shut from joy and kindly air
Heaven, descending in a vision
Taught my soul to do and bear –

It was night, a night of winter;
I lay on the dungeon floor,
And all other sounds were silent –
All, except the river's roar –

Over Death, and Desolation,
Fireless hearths, and lifeless homes
Over orphans' heart-sick sorrows,
Over fathers' bloody tombs;

Over friends that my arms never
Might embrace, in love again –
Memory pondered until madness
Struck its poignard in my brain –

Deepest slumber followed raving
Yet, methought, I brooded still
Still I saw my country bleeding
Dying for a Tyrant's will –

Not because *my* bliss was blasted
Burned within, the avenging flame –
Not because my scattered kindred
Died in woe, or lived in shame

God doth know, I would have given
Every bosom dear to me
Could that sacrifice have purchased
Tortured Gondal's liberty!

But, that at Ambition's bidding
All her cherished hopes should wane;
That her noblest sons should muster,
Strive, and fight and fall in vain –

Hut and castle, hall and cottage,
Roofless, crumbling to the ground –
Mighty Heaven, a glad Avenger
Thy eternal justice found!

Yes, the arm that once would shudder
Even to pierce a wounded deer,
I beheld it, unrelenting,
Choke in blood its sovereign's prayer –

Glorious dream! I saw the city
Blazing in imperial shine;
And among adoring thousands
Stood a man of form divine –

None need point the princely victim
Now he smiles with royal pride!
Now his glance is bright as lightning:
Now – the knife is in his side!

Ha, I saw how Death could darken –
Darken that triumphant eye!
His red heart's blood drenched my dagger;
My ear drank his dying sigh!

Shadows come! What means this midnight?
O my God, I know it all!
Know the fever-dream is over;
Unavenged the Avengers fall!

'TWAS ONE OF THOSE

'Twas one of those dark cloudy days
That sometimes come in summer's blaze
When heaven drops not when earth is still
And deeper green is on the hill

STILL AS SHE LOOKED

Still as she looked the iron clouds
Would part and sunlight shone between
But drearily strange and pale and cold

FALL LEAVES FALL

Fall leaves fall die flowers away
Lengthen night and shorten day
Every leaf speaks bliss to me
Fluttering from the autumn tree
I shall smile when wreaths of snow
Blossom where the rose should grow
I shall sing when night's decay
Ushers in a drearier day

SONG BY J. BRENZAIDA TO G.S.

I knew not 'twas so dire a crime
To say the word, Adieu:
But this shall be the only time
My slighted heart shall sue.

The wild moorside, the winter morn,
The gnarled and ancient tree –
If in your breast they waken scorn
Shall wake the same in me.

I can forget black eyes and brows
And lips of rosy charm
If you forget the sacred vows
Those faithless lips could form –

If hard commands can tame your love,
Or prison walls can hold
I would not wish to grieve above
A thing so false and cold –

And there are bosoms bound to mine
With links both tried and strong;
And there are eyes whose lightning shine
Has warmed and blessed me long:

Those eyes shall make my only day,
Shall set my spirit free
And chase the foolish thoughts away
That mourn your memory!

O COME WITH ME

O come with me thus ran the song
The moon is bright in Autumn's sky
And thou hast toiled and laboured long
With aching head and weary eye

O DREAM

O Dream, where art thou now?
Long years have past away
Since last, from off thine angel brow
I saw the light decay –

Alas, alas for me
Thou wert so bright and fair,
I could not think thy memory
Would yield me nought but care!

The sun-beam and the storm,
The summer-eve divine,
The silent night of solemn calm,
The full moon's cloudless shine

Were once entwined with thee
But now, with weary pain –
Lost vision! 'tis enough for me –
Thou canst not shine again –

LOUD WITHOUT THE WIND

Loud without the wind was roaring
   Through the waned Autumnal sky,
Drenching wet, the cold rain pouring
   Spoke of stormy winters nigh.

   All too like that dreary eve
   Sighed within repining grief –
   Sighed at first – but sighed not long
   Sweet – How softly sweet it came!
   Wild words of an ancient song –
   Undefined, without a name –

'It was spring, for the skylark was singing.'
Those words they awakened a spell –
They unlocked a deep fountain whose springing
Nor Absence nor Distance can quell.

In the gloom of a cloudy November
They uttered the music of May –
They kindled the perishing ember
Into fervour that could not decay

Awaken on all my dear moorlands
The wind in its glory and pride!
O call me from valleys and highlands
To walk by the hill-river's side!

It is swelled with the first snowy weather;
The rocks they are icy and hoar
And darker waves round the long heather
And the fern-leaves are sunny no more

There are no yellow-stars on the mountain,
The blue bells have long died away
From the brink of the moss-bedded fountain,
From the side of the wintery brae –

But lovelier than corn-fields all waving
In emerald and scarlet and gold
Are the slopes where the north-wind is raving
And the glens where I wandered of old –

'It was morning; the bright sun was beaming.'
How sweetly that brought back to me
The time when nor labour nor dreaming
Broke the sleep of the happy and free

But blithely we rose as the dusk heaven
Was melting to amber and blue –
And swift were the wings to our feet given
While we traversed the meadows of dew.

For the moors, for the moors where the short grass
Like velvet beneath us should lie!
For the moors, for the moors where each high pass
Rose sunny against the clear sky!

For the moors, where the linnet was trilling
Its song on the old granite stone –
Where the lark – the wild skylark was filling
Every breast with delight like its own.

What language can utter the feeling
That rose when, in exile afar,
On the brow of a lonely hill kneeling
I saw the brown heath growing there.

It was scattered and stunted, and told me
That soon even that would be gone
It whispered, 'The grim walls enfold me
I have bloomed in my last summer's sun'

But not the loved music whose waking
Makes the soul of the Swiss die away
Has a spell more adored and heart-breaking
Than in its half-blighted bells lay –

The spirit that bent 'neath its power
How it longed, how it burned to be free!
If I could have wept in that hour
Those tears had been heaven to me –

Well, well the sad minutes are moving
Though loaded with trouble and pain –
And sometime the loved and the loving
Shall meet on the mountains again –

A LITTLE WHILE

A little while, a little while
The noisy crowd are barred away;
And I can sing and I can smile
A little while I've holiday!

Where wilt thou go my harassed heart?
Full many a land invites thee now;
And places near, and far apart
Have rest for thee, my weary brow –

There is a spot 'mid barren hills
Where winter howls and driving rain
But if the dreary tempest chills
There is a light that warms again

The house is old, the trees are bare
And moonless bends the misty dome
But what on earth is half so dear –
So longed for as the hearth of home?

The mute bird sitting on the stone,
The dank moss dripping from the wall,
The garden-walk with weeds o'ergrown
I love them – how I love them all!

Shall I go there? or shall I seek
Another clime, another sky.
Where tongues familiar music speak
In accents dear to memory?

Yes, as I mused, the naked room,
The flickering firelight died away
And from the midst of cheerless gloom
I passed to bright, unclouded day –

A little and a lone green lane
That opened on a common wide
A distant, dreamy, dim blue chain
Of mountains circling every side –

A heaven so clear, an earth so calm,
So sweet, so soft, so hushed an air
And, deepening still the dreamlike charm,
Wild moor-sheep feeding everywhere –

That was the scene – I knew it well
I knew the pathways far and near
That winding o'er each billowy swell
Marked out the tracks of wandering deer

Could I have lingered but an hour
It well had paid a week of toil
But truth has banished fancy's power
I hear my dungeon bars recoil –

Even as I stood with raptured eye
Absorbed in bliss so deep and dear
My hour of rest had fleeted by
And given me back to weary care –

HOW STILL

How still, how happy! those are words
That once would scarce agree together
I loved the plashing of the surge –
The changing heaven the breezy weather,

More than smooth seas and cloudless skies
And solemn, soothing, softened airs
That in the forest woke no sighs
And from the green spray shook no tears

How still, how happy! now I feel
Where silence dwells is sweeter far
Than laughing mirth's most joyous swell
However pure its raptures are

Come sit down on this sunny stone
'Tis wintery light o'er flowerless moors –
But sit – for we are all alone
And clear expand heaven's breathless shores

I could think in the withered grass
Spring's budding wreaths we might discern
The violet's eye might shyly flash
And young leaves shoot among the fern

It is but thought – full many a night
The snow shall clothe those hills afar
And storms shall add a drearier blight
And winds shall wage a wilder war

Before the lark may herald in
Fresh foliage twined with blossoms fair
And summer days again begin
Their glory-haloed crown to wear

Yet my heart loves December's smile
As much as July's golden beam
Then let us sit and watch the while
The blue ice curdling on the stream –

I KNOW NOT HOW

I know not how it falls on me
This summer evening, hushed and lone
Yet the faint wind comes soothingly
With something of an olden tone

Forgive me if I've shunned so long
Your gentle greeting earth and air
But sorrow withers even the strong
And who can fight against despair

MONTH AFTER MONTH

Month after month year after year
My harp has poured a dreary strain –
At length a livelier note shall cheer
And pleasure tune its chords again

What though the stars and fair moonlight
Are quenched in morning dull and grey
They were but tokens of the night
And *this* my soul is day

MILD THE MIST

Mild the mist upon the hill
Telling not of storms tomorrow
No the day has wept its fill
Spent its store of silent sorrow

Oh I'm gone back to the days of youth
I am a child once more
And 'neath my father's sheltering roof
And near the old hall door

I watch this cloudy evening fall
After a day of rain
Blue mists sweet mists of summer pall
The horizon's mountain chain

The damp stands in the long green grass
As thick as morning's tears
And dreamy scents of fragrance pass
That breathe of other years

THE WIND WAS ROUGH

The wind was rough which tore
That leaf from its parent tree
The fate was cruel which bore
The withering corpse to me

We wander on we have no rest
It is a dreary way

What shadow is it
That ever moves before my eyes
It has a brow of ghostly whiteness

COME, WALK WITH ME

Come, walk with me,
There's only thee
To bless my spirit now –
We used to love on winter nights
To wander through the snow;
Can we not woo back old delights?
The clouds rush dark and wild
They fleck with shade our mountain heights
The same as long ago
And on the horizon rest at last
In looming masses piled;
While moonbeams flash and fly so fast
We scarce can say they smiled –

Come walk with me, come walk with me;
We were not once so few
But Death has stolen our company
As sunshine steals the dew –
He took them one by one and we
Are left the only two;
So closer would my feelings twine
Because they have no stay but thine –

'Nay call me not – it may not be
Is human love so true?
Can Friendship's flower droop on for years
And then revive anew?
No, though the soil be wet with tears,
How fair soe'er it grew
The vital sap once perished
Will never flow again
And surer than that dwelling dread,
The narrow dungeon of the dead
Time parts the hearts of men – '

IT IS TOO LATE

It is too late to call thee now –
I will not nurse that dream again
For every joy that lit my brow
Would bring its after-storm of pain –

Besides the mist is half withdrawn,
The barren mountain-side lies bare
And sunshine and awaking morn
Paint no more golden visions there –

Yet ever in my grateful breast
Thy darling shade shall cherished be
For God alone doth know how blest
My early years have been in thee!

IF GRIEF FOR GRIEF

If grief for grief can touch thee,
If answering woe for woe,
If any ruth can melt thee
Come to me now!

I cannot be more lonely,
More drear I cannot be!
My worn heart throbs so wildly
'Twill break for thee –

And when the world despises –
When heaven repels my prayer –
Will not mine angel comfort?
Mine idol hear?

Yes by the tears I've poured,
By all my hours of pain
O I shall surely win thee
Beloved, again!

THE NIGHT-WIND

In summer's mellow midnight
A cloudless moon shone through
Our open parlour window
And rosetrees wet with dew

I sat in silent musing –
The soft wind waved my hair
It told me Heaven was glorious
And sleeping Earth was fair –

I needed not its breathing
To bring such thoughts to me
But still it whispered lowly
'How dark the woods will be! –

'The thick leaves in my murmur
Are rustling like a dream,
And all their myriad voices
Instinct with spirit seem'

I said, 'Go gentle singer,
Thy wooing voice is kind
But do not think its music
Has power to reach my mind –

'Play with the scented flower,
The young tree's supple bough –
And leave my human feelings
In their own course to flow'

The Wanderer would not leave me
Its kiss grew warmer still –
'O come,' it sighed so sweetly
'I'll win thee 'gainst thy will –

'Have we not been from childhood friends?
Have I not loved thee long?
As long as thou hast loved the night
Whose silence wakes my song?

'And when thy heart is laid at rest
Beneath the church-yard stone
I shall have time enough to mourn
And thou to be alone' –

I SEE AROUND ME

I see around me tombstones grey
Stretching their shadow far away.
Beneath the turf my footsteps tread
Lie low and lone the silent dead –
Beneath the turf – beneath the mould –
Forever dark, forever cold –
And my eyes cannot hold the tears
That memory hoards from vanished years
For Time and Death and Mortal pain
Give wounds that will not heal again –
Let me remember half the woe
I've seen and heard and felt below
And heaven itself – so pure and blest
Could never give my spirit rest –
Sweet land of light! thy children fair
Know nought akin to our despair –
Nor have they felt, nor can they tell
What tenants haunt each mortal cell
What gloomy guests we hold within –
Torments and madness, tears and sin!
Well – may they live in ecstasy
Their long eternity of joy;
At least we would not bring them down
With us to weep, with us to groan,
No – Earth would wish no other sphere
To taste her cup of sufferings drear;
She turns from Heaven a careless eye

And only mourns that *we* must die!
Ah mother, what shall comfort thee
In all this boundless misery?
To cheer our eager eyes a while
We see thee smile, how fondly smile!
But who reads not through that tender glow
Thy deep, unutterable woe?
Indeed no dazzling land above
Can cheat thee of thy children's love –
We all in life's departing shine
Our last dear longings blend with thine;
And struggle still, and strive to trace
With clouded gaze thy darling face
We would not leave our native home
For *any* world beyond the Tomb
No – rather on thy kindly breast
Let us be laid in lasting rest
Or waken but to share with thee
A mutual immortality –

WRITTEN IN ASPIN CASTLE

How do I love on summer nights
To sit within this Norman door
Whose sombre portal hides the lights
Thickening above me evermore!

How do I love to hear the flow
Of Aspin's water murmuring low
And hours long listen to the breeze
That sighs in Rockden's waving trees

Tonight, there is no wind to wake
One ripple on the lonely lake –
Tonight the clouds subdued and grey
Starlight and moonlight shut away

'Tis calm and still and almost drear
So utter is the solitude;
But still I love to linger here
And form my mood to nature's mood –

There's a wild walk beneath the rocks
Following the bend of Aspin's side
'Tis worn by feet of mountain-flocks
That wander down to drink the tide

Never by cliff and gnarled tree
Wound fairy path so sweet to me
Yet of the native shepherds none
In open day and cheerful sun
Will tread its labyrinths alone

Far less when evening's pensive hour
Hushes the bird and shuts the flower
And gives to Fancy magic power
O'er each familiar tone.

For round their hearths they'll tell the tale
And every listener swears it true
How wanders there a phantom pale
With spirit-eyes of dreamy blue –

It always walks with head declined
Its long curls move not in the wind
Its face is fair – divinely fair;
But brooding on that angel brow
Rests such a shade of deep despair
As nought divine could ever know

How oft in twilight lingering lone
I've stood to watch that phantom rise
And seen in mist and moonlit stone
Its gleaming hair and solemn eyes

The ancient men in secret say
'Tis the first chief of Aspin grey
That haunts his feudal home

But why, around that alien grave
Three thousand miles beyond the wave –
Where his exiled ashes lie
Under the cope of England's sky –
Doth he not rather roam?

I've seen his picture in the hall;
It hangs upon an eastern wall
And often when the sun declines
That picture like an angel shines –

And when the moonbeam chill and blue
Streams the spectral windows through
That picture's like a spectre too –

The hall is full of portraits rare;
Beauty and mystery mingle there –
At his right hand an infant fair
Looks from its golden frame –

And just like his its ringlets bright
Its large dark eye of shadowy light
Its cheek's pure hue, its forehead white
And like its noble name –

Daughter divine! and could his gaze
Fall coldly on thy peerless face?
And did he never smile to see
Himself restored to infancy?

Never part back that golden flow
Of curls, and kiss that pearly brow
And feel no other earthly bliss
Was equal to that parent's kiss?

No; turn towards the western side
There stands Sidonia's deity!
In all her glory, all her pride!
And truly like a god she seems
Some god of wild enthusiast's dreams
And this is she for whom he died!
For whom his spirit unforgiven,
Wanders unsheltered shut from heaven
An outcast for eternity –

Those eyes are dust – those lips are clay –
That form is mouldered all away
Nor thought, nor sense, nor pulse, nor breath
The whole devoured and lost in death!

There is no worm, however mean,
That living, is not nobler now
Than she – Lord Alfred's idol queen
So loved – so worshipped long ago –

O come away! the Norman door
Is silvered with a sudden shine –
Come leave these dreams o'er things of yore
And turn to Nature's face divine –

O'er wood and wold, o'er flood and fell
O'er flashing lake and gleaming dell
The harvest moon looks down

And when heaven smiles with love and light
And earth looks back so dazzling bright
In such a scene, on such a night
Earth's children should not frown –

HAD THERE BEEN FALSEHOOD

Had there been falsehood in my breast
No thorns had marred my road
This spirit had not lost its rest
These tears had never flowed

ALL DAY I'VE TOILED

All day I've toiled but not with pain
In learning's golden mine
And now at eventide again
The moonbeams softly shine

There is no snow upon the ground
No frost on wind or wave
The south wind blew with gentlest sound
And broke their icy grave

'Tis sweet to wander here at night
To watch the winter die
With heart as summer sunshine light
And warm as summer's sky

O may I never lose the peace
That lulls me gently now
Though time should change my youthful face
And years should shade my brow

True to myself and true to all
May I be healthful still
And turn away from passion's call
And curb my own wild will

WHAT WINTER FLOODS

What winter floods what showers of spring
Have drenched the grass by night and day
And yet beneath that spectre ring
Unmoved and undiscovered lay

A mute remembrancer of crime
Long lost concealed forgot for years
It comes at last to cancel time
And waken unavailing tears

ALL HUSHED AND STILL

All hushed and still within the house
Without – all wind and driving rain
But something whispers to my mind
Through rain and through the wailing wind
      – Never again
Never again? Why not again?
Memory has power as real as thine

SHE DRIED HER TEARS

She dried her tears and they did smile
To see her cheeks' returning glow
How little dreaming all the while
That full heart throbbed to overflow

With that sweet look and lively tone
And bright eye shining all the day
They could not guess at midnight lone
How she would weep the time away

NO COWARD SOUL

No coward soul is mine
No trembler in the world's storm-troubled sphere
I see Heaven's glories shine
And Faith shines equal arming me from Fear

O God within my breast
Almighty ever-present Deity
Life, that in me hast rest
As I Undying Life, have power in thee

Vain are the thousand creeds
That move men's hearts, unutterably vain,
Worthless as withered weeds
Or idlest froth amid the boundless main

To waken doubt in one
Holding so fast by thy infinity
So surely anchored on
The steadfast rock of Immortality

With wide-embracing love
Thy spirit animates eternal years
Pervades and broods above,
Changes, sustains, dissolves, creates and rears

Though Earth and moon were gone
And suns and universes ceased to be
And thou wert left alone
Every Existence would exist in thee

There is not room for Death
Nor atom that his might could render void
Since thou art Being and Breath
And what thou art may never be destroyed